Pebble®
Plus

Monkeys

Baboons

by Cecilia Pinto McCarthy

Consulting Editor: Gail Saunders-Smith, PhD

Consultant: Lori Perkins,
Vice President of Collections
Zoo Atlanta, Atlanta, Georgia

CAPSTONE PRESS
a capstone imprint

Pebble Plus is published by Capstone Press,
1710 Roe Crest Drive, North Mankato, Minnesota 56003
www.capstonepub.com

Library of Congress Cataloging-in-Publication Data
Cataloging-in-publication information is on file with the Library of Congress.
ISBN 978-1-62065-109-4 (library binding)
ISBN 978-1-4765-1078-1 (ebook PDF)

Editorial Credits
Christopher L. Harbo, editor; Bobbie Nuytten, designer; Svetlana Zhurkin, media researcher;
Eric Manske, production specialist

Photo Credits
Biosphoto: Sylvie Bergerot & Eric Robert, 21; Dreamstime: Andrevaladao, 9, Frank De Villiers, 15, Jurie Maree, 19, Steffen Foerster, 5; Shutterstock: Dennis Donohue, 13, Iv Nikolny, 17, Matt Gibson, 11, Steffen Foerster Photography, cover, 1, Vadim Petrakov, 7

Note to Parents and Teachers

The Monkeys set supports national science standards related to life science. This book describes and illustrates baboons. The images support early readers in understanding the text. The repetition of words and phrases helps early readers learn new words. This book also introduces early readers to subject-specific vocabulary words, which are defined in the Glossary section. Early readers may need assistance to read some words and to use the Table of Contents, Glossary, Read More, Internet Sites, and Index sections of the book.

Printed in the United States of America in North Mankato, Minnesota.
092012   006933CGS13

Table of Contents

Doglike Monkey

They have long snouts

and sharp canine teeth.

They walk on all fours.

No, they're not dogs.

They are baboons.

Most baboons live in hot African grasslands and forests. Hamadryas baboons live on rocky cliffs in northeastern Africa, Saudi Arabia, and Yemen.

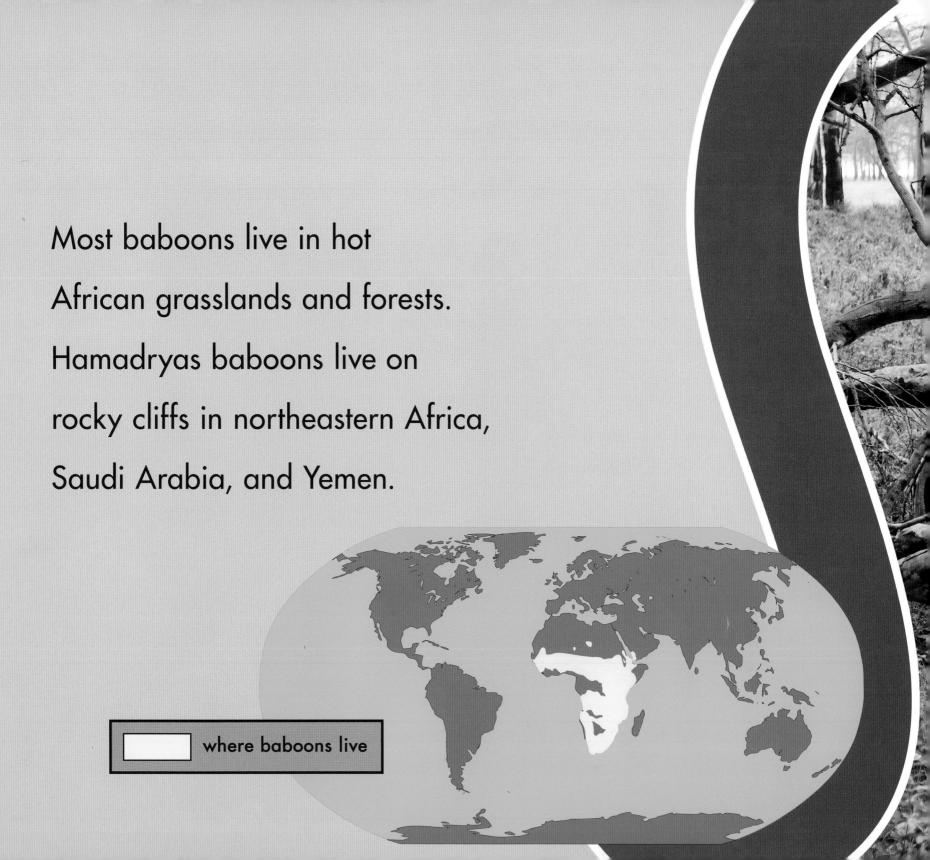

where baboons live

Baboon Bodies

Baboons are covered with rough fur, except on their faces and bottoms. Most males have thick fur on their necks and shoulders.

Baboons grow to different sizes.

Chacma baboons weigh

up to 90 pounds (41 kilograms).

Guinea baboons weigh as little

as 30 pounds (14 kg).

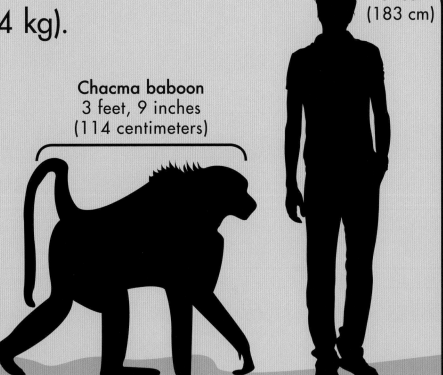

Chacma baboon
3 feet, 9 inches
(114 centimeters)

6 feet
(183 cm)

Finding Food

Baboons spend cool mornings eating fruits, plants, and insects. They stuff their cheek pouches with food to eat later.

Growing Up

Female baboons give birth

to one baby every two years.

Infants have pink skin,

dark fur, and big ears.

They cling to their mothers' chests.

Older infants ride piggy-back.

At about age five, males leave

and join another baboon group.

In the wild, baboons live

about 25 to 30 years.

Living in Troops

About 50 to 100 baboons live in groups called troops. Baboons spend hours grooming. Cleaning each other's fur helps baboons bond.

Troops of baboons use sounds to talk and stay safe from leopards and chimpanzees. Wahoo! This bark tells other baboons that danger is near.

Glossary

bond—to form a close friendship with someone

canine—a long, pointed tooth

cling—to hold on tightly

grassland—a large, open area where grass and low plants grow

groom—to clean and keep neat

infant—a very young animal

pouch—a part of the body shaped like a bag

snout—the long, front part of an animal's head

troop—a group

Read More

Borgert-Spaniol, Megan. *Baboons*. Animal Safari. Minneapolis: Bellwether Media, Inc., 2013.

Gosman, Gillian. *Baboons*. Monkey Business. New York: PowerKids Press, 2012.

Spilsbury, Louise. *Baboon*. A Day in the Life: Grassland Animals. Chicago: Heinemann Library, 2011.

Walden, Katherine. *Baboons*. Safari Animals. New York: Rosen Pub. Group's PowerKids Press, 2009.

Internet Sites

FactHound offers a safe, fun way to find Internet sites related to this book. All of the sites on FactHound have been researched by our staff.

Here's all you do:

Visit *www.facthound.com*

Type in this code: 9781620651094

Index

Word Count: 202
Grade: 1
Early-Intervention Level: 16